# PATHFYNDER JOURNAL

Copyright © 2023 by Erinn Watkins

All Rights Reserved.

No part of this book may be used or reproduced, distributed, or transmitted in any form by any means, including photocopying, recording, taping, by any information storage retrieval system, or other electronic or mechanical methods, without the prior written permission of the publisher or author, except as permitted by U.S. copyright law.

Book Cover by Eric Watkins

ISBN: 979-8-9885185-3-2 - PathfYnder Journal

First Printing, 2023

3 4 5 6 7 8 9 10 11 12 13 14 15 16 17 18 19 20 21 22 23 24 25 26 27 28 29 30 31
JAN FEB MAR APR MAY JUN JUL AUG SEP OCT NOV DEC
Sunday Monday Tuesday Wednesday Thursday Friday Saturday

**Live well and be your best self.**

1 2 3 4 5 6 7 8 9 10 11 12 13 14 15 16 17 18 19 20 21 22 23 24 25 26 27 28 29 30
JAN FEB MAR APR MAY JUN JUL AUG SEP OCT NOV DEC
Sunday Monday Tuesday Wednesday Thursday Friday Saturday

**Have faith in yourself and your abilities.**

3 4 5 6 7 8 9 10 11 12 13 14 15 16 17 18 19 20 21 22 23 24 25 26 27 28 29 30 31
JAN FEB MAR APR MAY JUN JUL AUG SEP OCT NOV DEC
Sunday Monday Tuesday Wednesday Thursday Friday Saturday

**Smile, even when you don't want to.**

1 2 3 4 5 6 7 8 9 10 11 12 13 14 15 16 17 18 19 20 21 22 23 24 25 26 27 28 29 30 31
JAN FEB MAR APR MAY JUN JUL AUG SEP OCT NOV DEC
Sunday Monday Tuesday Wednesday Thursday Friday Saturday

**Ask for help and learn to accept help.**

3 4 5 6 7 8 9 10 11 12 13 14 15 16 17 18 19 20 21 22 23 24 25 26 27 28 29 30 31
JAN FEB MAR APR MAY JUN JUL AUG SEP OCT NOV DEC
Sunday Monday Tuesday Wednesday Thursday Friday Saturday

When you choose your path, you get everything that goes with it.

1 2 3 4 5 6 7 8 9 10 11 12 13 14 15 16 17 18 19 20 21 22 23 24 25 26 27 28 29 30
JAN FEB MAR APR MAY JUN JUL AUG SEP OCT NOV DEC
Sunday Monday Tuesday Wednesday Thursday Friday Saturday

**Never take ownership of things that don't belong to you.**

3 4 5 6 7 8 9 10 11 12 13 14 15 16 17 18 19 20 21 22 23 24 25 26 27 28 29 30 31
JAN FEB MAR APR MAY JUN JUL AUG SEP OCT NOV DEC
Sunday Monday Tuesday Wednesday Thursday Friday Saturday

**Be patient.**

1 2 3 4 5 6 7 8 9 10 11 12 13 14 15 16 17 18 19 20 21 22 23 24 25 26 27 28 29 30 31
JAN FEB MAR APR MAY JUN JUL AUG SEP OCT NOV DEC
Sunday Monday Tuesday Wednesday Thursday Friday Saturday

**Learn how to take a joke.**

3 4 5 6 7 8 9 10 11 12 13 14 15 16 17 18 19 20 21 22 23 24 25 26 27 28 29 30 31
JAN FEB MAR APR MAY JUN JUL AUG SEP OCT NOV DEC
Sunday Monday Tuesday Wednesday Thursday Friday Saturday

**Recognize sarcasm.**

1 2 3 4 5 6 7 8 9 10 11 12 13 14 15 16 17 18 19 20 21 22 23 24 25 26 27 28 29 30
JAN FEB MAR APR MAY JUN JUL AUG SEP OCT NOV DEC
Sunday Monday Tuesday Wednesday Thursday Friday Saturday

**The "what" is more important than the "why".**

3 4 5 6 7 8 9 10 11 12 13 14 15 16 17 18 19 20 21 22 23 24 25 26 27 28 29 30 31
JAN  FEB  MAR  APR  MAY  JUN  JUL  AUG  SEP  OCT  NOV  DEC
Sunday  Monday  Tuesday  Wednesday  Thursday  Friday  Saturday

**Identify action items.**

1 2 3 4 5 6 7 8 9 10 11 12 13 14 15 16 17 18 19 20 21 22 23 24 25 26 27 28 29 30
JAN FEB MAR APR MAY JUN JUL AUG SEP OCT NOV DEC
Sunday Monday Tuesday Wednesday Thursday Friday Saturday

**Learn to stand alone.**

3 4 5 6 7 8 9 10 11 12 13 14 15 16 17 18 19 20 21 22 23 24 25 26 27 28 29 30 31
JAN FEB MAR APR MAY JUN JUL AUG SEP OCT NOV DEC
Sunday Monday Tuesday Wednesday Thursday Friday Saturday

**Think outside the box.**

1 2 3 4 5 6 7 8 9 10 11 12 13 14 15 16 17 18 19 20 21 22 23 24 25 26 27 28 29 30
JAN FEB MAR APR MAY JUN JUL AUG SEP OCT NOV DEC
Sunday Monday Tuesday Wednesday Thursday Friday Saturday

**Assume the positive...the first time.**

3 4 5 6 7 8 9 10 11 12 13 14 15 16 17 18 19 20 21 22 23 24 25 26 27 28 29 30 31
JAN FEB MAR APR MAY JUN JUL AUG SEP OCT NOV DEC
Sunday Monday Tuesday Wednesday Thursday Friday Saturday

**Never go along to get along.**

1 2 3 4 5 6 7 8 9 10 11 12 13 14 15 16 17 18 19 20 21 22 23 24 25 26 27 28 29 30 31
JAN FEB MAR APR MAY JUN JUL AUG SEP OCT NOV DEC
Sunday Monday Tuesday Wednesday Thursday Friday Saturday

**Understand where people are coming from.**

3 4 5 6 7 8 9 10 11 12 13 14 15 16 17 18 19 20 21 22 23 24 25 26 27 28 29 30 31
JAN FEB MAR APR MAY JUN JUL AUG SEP OCT NOV DEC
Sunday Monday Tuesday Wednesday Thursday Friday Saturday

**You don't always have to be right.**

1 2 3 4 5 6 7 8 9 10 11 12 13 14 15 16 17 18 19 20 21 22 23 24 25 26 27 28 29 30
JAN FEB MAR APR MAY JUN JUL AUG SEP OCT NOV DEC
Sunday Monday Tuesday Wednesday Thursday Friday Saturday

**You can both be right.**

3 4 5 6 7 8 9 10 11 12 13 14 15 16 17 18 19 20 21 22 23 24 25 26 27 28 29 30 31
JAN FEB MAR APR MAY JUN JUL AUG SEP OCT NOV DEC
Sunday Monday Tuesday Wednesday Thursday Friday Saturday

**Focus on commonalities instead of differences.**

1 2 3 4 5 6 7 8 9 10 11 12 13 14 15 16 17 18 19 20 21 22 23 24 25 26 27 28 29 30 31

JAN  FEB  MAR  APR  MAY  JUN  JUL  AUG  SEP  OCT  NOV  DEC

Sunday  Monday  Tuesday  Wednesday  Thursday  Friday  Saturday

**Practice being kind to yourself.**

3 4 5 6 7 8 9 10 11 12 13 14 15 16 17 18 19 20 21 22 23 24 25 26 27 28 29 30 31
JAN FEB MAR APR MAY JUN JUL AUG SEP OCT NOV DEC
Sunday Monday Tuesday Wednesday Thursday Friday Saturday

**Rehearse how to deal with stressful situations.**

1 2 3 4 5 6 7 8 9 10 11 12 13 14 15 16 17 18 19 20 21 22 23 24 25 26 27 28 29 30
JAN  FEB  MAR  APR  MAY  JUN  JUL  AUG  SEP  OCT  NOV  DEC
Sunday  Monday  Tuesday  Wednesday  Thursday  Friday  Saturday

**Everything does not deserve a reply.**

3 4 5 6 7 8 9 10 11 12 13 14 15 16 17 18 19 20 21 22 23 24 25 26 27 28 29 30 31
JAN FEB MAR APR MAY JUN JUL AUG SEP OCT NOV DEC
Sunday Monday Tuesday Wednesday Thursday Friday Saturday

**Everyone does not deserve an apology.**

1 2 3 4 5 6 7 8 9 10 11 12 13 14 15 16 17 18 19 20 21 22 23 24 25 26 27 28 29 30

JAN  FEB  MAR  APR  MAY  JUN  JUL  AUG  SEP  OCT  NOV  DEC

Sunday  Monday  Tuesday  Wednesday  Thursday  Friday  Saturday

**Everything is not an insult.**

3 4 5 6 7 8 9 10 11 12 13 14 15 16 17 18 19 20 21 22 23 24 25 26 27 28 29 30 31
JAN  FEB  MAR  APR  MAY  JUN  JUL  AUG  SEP  OCT  NOV  DEC
Sunday  Monday  Tuesday  Wednesday  Thursday  Friday  Saturday

**You don't have to forgive everyone.
You can make peace with them instead.**

1 2 3 4 5 6 7 8 9 10 11 12 13 14 15 16 17 18 19 20 21 22 23 24 25 26 27 28 29 30
JAN FEB MAR APR MAY JUN JUL AUG SEP OCT NOV DEC
Sunday Monday Tuesday Wednesday Thursday Friday Saturday

**You don't have to change minds.
Just defend your position.**

3 4 5 6 7 8 9 10 11 12 13 14 15 16 17 18 19 20 21 22 23 24 25 26 27 28 29 30 31
JAN  FEB  MAR  APR  MAY  JUN  JUL  AUG  SEP  OCT  NOV  DEC
Sunday  Monday  Tuesday  Wednesday  Thursday  Friday  Saturday

**Recognize how different people send and receive information.**

1 2 3 4 5 6 7 8 9 10 11 12 13 14 15 16 17 18 19 20 21 22 23 24 25 26 27 28 29 30
JAN FEB MAR APR MAY JUN JUL AUG SEP OCT NOV DEC
Sunday Monday Tuesday Wednesday Thursday Friday Saturday

**Sometimes be unpredictable.**

3 4 5 6 7 8 9 10 11 12 13 14 15 16 17 18 19 20 21 22 23 24 25 26 27 28 29 30 31
JAN  FEB  MAR  APR  MAY  JUN  JUL  AUG  SEP  OCT  NOV  DEC
Sunday  Monday  Tuesday  Wednesday  Thursday  Friday  Saturday

**Find your "step one".**

1 2 3 4 5 6 7 8 9 10 11 12 13 14 15 16 17 18 19 20 21 22 23 24 25 26 27 28 29 30

JAN FEB MAR APR MAY JUN JUL AUG SEP OCT NOV DEC

Sunday Monday Tuesday Wednesday Thursday Friday Saturday

_____

_____

_____

_____

_____

_____

_____

_____

_____

_____

_____

_____

_____

_____

**Recognize the difference between facts and emotions.**

3 4 5 6 7 8 9 10 11 12 13 14 15 16 17 18 19 20 21 22 23 24 25 26 27 28 29 30 31

JAN  FEB  MAR  APR  MAY  JUN  JUL  AUG  SEP  OCT  NOV  DEC

Sunday  Monday  Tuesday  Wednesday  Thursday  Friday  Saturday

**Never give anyone permission to make you feel sad or inferior.**

1 2 3 4 5 6 7 8 9 10 11 12 13 14 15 16 17 18 19 20 21 22 23 24 25 26 27 28 29 30
JAN FEB MAR APR MAY JUN JUL AUG SEP OCT NOV DEC
Sunday Monday Tuesday Wednesday Thursday Friday Saturday

_____

_____

_____

_____

_____

_____

_____

_____

_____

_____

_____

_____

_____

_____

_____

_____

_____

**Take responsibility for your actions.**

3 4 5 6 7 8 9 10 11 12 13 14 15 16 17 18 19 20 21 22 23 24 25 26 27 28 29 30 31
JAN FEB MAR APR MAY JUN JUL AUG SEP OCT NOV DEC
Sunday Monday Tuesday Wednesday Thursday Friday Saturday

**Be a leader when no one else will.**

1 2 3 4 5 6 7 8 9 10 11 12 13 14 15 16 17 18 19 20 21 22 23 24 25 26 27 28 29 30
JAN FEB MAR APR MAY JUN JUL AUG SEP OCT NOV DEC
Sunday Monday Tuesday Wednesday Thursday Friday Saturday

**Be a good follower.**

3 4 5 6 7 8 9 10 11 12 13 14 15 16 17 18 19 20 21 22 23 24 25 26 27 28 29 30 31
JAN  FEB  MAR  APR  MAY  JUN  JUL  AUG  SEP  OCT  NOV  DEC
Sunday  Monday  Tuesday  Wednesday  Thursday  Friday  Saturday

**Don't repeat the same mistake.**

1 2 3 4 5 6 7 8 9 10 11 12 13 14 15 16 17 18 19 20 21 22 23 24 25 26 27 28 29 30
JAN FEB MAR APR MAY JUN JUL AUG SEP OCT NOV DEC
Sunday Monday Tuesday Wednesday Thursday Friday Saturday

**Be honest with yourself and others.**

3 4 5 6 7 8 9 10 11 12 13 14 15 16 17 18 19 20 21 22 23 24 25 26 27 28 29 30 31
JAN FEB MAR APR MAY JUN JUL AUG SEP OCT NOV DEC
Sunday Monday Tuesday Wednesday Thursday Friday Saturday

**Have integrity.**

1 2 3 4 5 6 7 8 9 10 11 12 13 14 15 16 17 18 19 20 21 22 23 24 25 26 27 28 29 30
JAN FEB MAR APR MAY JUN JUL AUG SEP OCT NOV DEC
Sunday Monday Tuesday Wednesday Thursday Friday Saturday

**Behave in honor even when no one is watching.**

3 4 5 6 7 8 9 10 11 12 13 14 15 16 17 18 19 20 21 22 23 24 25 26 27 28 29 30 31
JAN FEB MAR APR MAY JUN JUL AUG SEP OCT NOV DEC
Sunday Monday Tuesday Wednesday Thursday Friday Saturday

**Live by moral and ethical principles.**

1 2 3 4 5 6 7 8 9 10 11 12 13 14 15 16 17 18 19 20 21 22 23 24 25 26 27 28 29 30
JAN FEB MAR APR MAY JUN JUL AUG SEP OCT NOV DEC
Sunday Monday Tuesday Wednesday Thursday Friday Saturday

_____

_____

_____

_____

_____

_____

_____

_____

_____

_____

_____

_____

_____

_____

_____

_____

**Have personal courage: the ability to face
fear, danger, and adversity.**

3 4 5 6 7 8 9 10 11 12 13 14 15 16 17 18 19 20 21 22 23 24 25 26 27 28 29 30 31
JAN FEB MAR APR MAY JUN JUL AUG SEP OCT NOV DEC
Sunday Monday Tuesday Wednesday Thursday Friday Saturday

**Don't be afraid to be wrong.**

1 2 3 4 5 6 7 8 9 10 11 12 13 14 15 16 17 18 19 20 21 22 23 24 25 26 27 28 29 30
JAN FEB MAR APR MAY JUN JUL AUG SEP OCT NOV DEC
Sunday Monday Tuesday Wednesday Thursday Friday Saturday

**Don't be afraid to agree with an adversary.**

3 4 5 6 7 8 9 10 11 12 13 14 15 16 17 18 19 20 21 22 23 24 25 26 27 28 29 30 31
JAN  FEB  MAR  APR  MAY  JUN  JUL  AUG  SEP  OCT  NOV  DEC
Sunday  Monday  Tuesday  Wednesday  Thursday  Friday  Saturday

**Lead with a smile.**

1 2 3 4 5 6 7 8 9 10 11 12 13 14 15 16 17 18 19 20 21 22 23 24 25 26 27 28 29 30
JAN  FEB  MAR  APR  MAY  JUN  JUL  AUG  SEP  OCT  NOV  DEC
Sunday  Monday  Tuesday  Wednesday  Thursday  Friday  Saturday

**Never let anyone or anything steal your joy.**

3 4 5 6 7 8 9 10 11 12 13 14 15 16 17 18 19 20 21 22 23 24 25 26 27 28 29 30 31
JAN  FEB  MAR  APR  MAY  JUN  JUL  AUG  SEP  OCT  NOV  DEC
Sunday  Monday  Tuesday  Wednesday  Thursday  Friday  Saturday

**Live well and be your best self.**

1 2 3 4 5 6 7 8 9 10 11 12 13 14 15 16 17 18 19 20 21 22 23 24 25 26 27 28 29 30
JAN FEB MAR APR MAY JUN JUL AUG SEP OCT NOV DEC
Sunday Monday Tuesday Wednesday Thursday Friday Saturday

**Have faith in yourself and your abilities.**

3 4 5 6 7 8 9 10 11 12 13 14 15 16 17 18 19 20 21 22 23 24 25 26 27 28 29 30 31
JAN FEB MAR APR MAY JUN JUL AUG SEP OCT NOV DEC
Sunday  Monday  Tuesday  Wednesday  Thursday  Friday  Saturday

**Live well and be your best self.**

1 2 3 4 5 6 7 8 9 10 11 12 13 14 15 16 17 18 19 20 21 22 23 24 25 26 27 28 29 30
JAN FEB MAR APR MAY JUN JUL AUG SEP OCT NOV DEC
Sunday Monday Tuesday Wednesday Thursday Friday Saturday

**Have faith in yourself and your abilities.**

3 4 5 6 7 8 9 10 11 12 13 14 15 16 17 18 19 20 21 22 23 24 25 26 27 28 29 30 31
JAN FEB MAR APR MAY JUN JUL AUG SEP OCT NOV DEC
Sunday Monday Tuesday Wednesday Thursday Friday Saturday

**Smile, even when you don't want to.**

1 2 3 4 5 6 7 8 9 10 11 12 13 14 15 16 17 18 19 20 21 22 23 24 25 26 27 28 29 30
JAN FEB MAR APR MAY JUN JUL AUG SEP OCT NOV DEC
Sunday Monday Tuesday Wednesday Thursday Friday Saturday

**Ask for help and learn to accept help.**

3 4 5 6 7 8 9 10 11 12 13 14 15 16 17 18 19 20 21 22 23 24 25 26 27 28 29 30 31
JAN FEB MAR APR MAY JUN JUL AUG SEP OCT NOV DEC
Sunday Monday Tuesday Wednesday Thursday Friday Saturday

**When you choose your path, you get everything that goes with it.**

1 2 3 4 5 6 7 8 9 10 11 12 13 14 15 16 17 18 19 20 21 22 23 24 25 26 27 28 29 30

JAN FEB MAR APR MAY JUN JUL AUG SEP OCT NOV DEC

Sunday Monday Tuesday Wednesday Thursday Friday Saturday

**Never take ownership of things that don't belong to you.**

3 4 5 6 7 8 9 10 11 12 13 14 15 16 17 18 19 20 21 22 23 24 25 26 27 28 29 30 31
JAN FEB MAR APR MAY JUN JUL AUG SEP OCT NOV DEC
Sunday Monday Tuesday Wednesday Thursday Friday Saturday

**Be patient.**

1 2 3 4 5 6 7 8 9 10 11 12 13 14 15 16 17 18 19 20 21 22 23 24 25 26 27 28 29 30
JAN FEB MAR APR MAY JUN JUL AUG SEP OCT NOV DEC
Sunday Monday Tuesday Wednesday Thursday Friday Saturday

**Learn how to take a joke.**

3 4 5 6 7 8 9 10 11 12 13 14 15 16 17 18 19 20 21 22 23 24 25 26 27 28 29 30 31
JAN FEB MAR APR MAY JUN JUL AUG SEP OCT NOV DEC
Sunday Monday Tuesday Wednesday Thursday Friday Saturday

**Recognize sarcasm.**

1 2 3 4 5 6 7 8 9 10 11 12 13 14 15 16 17 18 19 20 21 22 23 24 25 26 27 28 29 30
JAN FEB MAR APR MAY JUN JUL AUG SEP OCT NOV DEC
Sunday Monday Tuesday Wednesday Thursday Friday Saturday

**The "what" is more important than the "why".**

3 4 5 6 7 8 9 10 11 12 13 14 15 16 17 18 19 20 21 22 23 24 25 26 27 28 29 30 31
JAN  FEB  MAR  APR  MAY  JUN  JUL  AUG  SEP  OCT  NOV  DEC
Sunday  Monday  Tuesday  Wednesday  Thursday  Friday  Saturday

**Identify action items.**

1 2 3 4 5 6 7 8 9 10 11 12 13 14 15 16 17 18 19 20 21 22 23 24 25 26 27 28 29 30
JAN FEB MAR APR MAY JUN JUL AUG SEP OCT NOV DEC
Sunday Monday Tuesday Wednesday Thursday Friday Saturday

_____

_____

_____

_____

_____

_____

_____

_____

_____

_____

_____

_____

_____

**Learn to stand alone.**

3 4 5 6 7 8 9 10 11 12 13 14 15 16 17 18 19 20 21 22 23 24 25 26 27 28 29 30 31
JAN FEB MAR APR MAY JUN JUL AUG SEP OCT NOV DEC
Sunday Monday Tuesday Wednesday Thursday Friday Saturday

**Think outside the box.**

1 2 3 4 5 6 7 8 9 10 11 12 13 14 15 16 17 18 19 20 21 22 23 24 25 26 27 28 29 30

JAN FEB MAR APR MAY JUN JUL AUG SEP OCT NOV DEC

Sunday Monday Tuesday Wednesday Thursday Friday Saturday

___

___

___

___

___

___

___

___

___

___

___

___

___

___

___

___

**Assume the positive...the first time.**

3 4 5 6 7 8 9 10 11 12 13 14 15 16 17 18 19 20 21 22 23 24 25 26 27 28 29 30 31
JAN FEB MAR APR MAY JUN JUL AUG SEP OCT NOV DEC
Sunday Monday Tuesday Wednesday Thursday Friday Saturday

**Never go along to get along.**

1 2 3 4 5 6 7 8 9 10 11 12 13 14 15 16 17 18 19 20 21 22 23 24 25 26 27 28 29 30
JAN FEB MAR APR MAY JUN JUL AUG SEP OCT NOV DEC
Sunday Monday Tuesday Wednesday Thursday Friday Saturday

_____

_____

_____

_____

_____

_____

_____

_____

_____

_____

_____

_____

_____

_____

_____

**Understand where people are coming from.**

3 4 5 6 7 8 9 10 11 12 13 14 15 16 17 18 19 20 21 22 23 24 25 26 27 28 29 30 31
JAN FEB MAR APR MAY JUN JUL AUG SEP OCT NOV DEC
Sunday Monday Tuesday Wednesday Thursday Friday Saturday

**You don't always have to be right.**

1 2 3 4 5 6 7 8 9 10 11 12 13 14 15 16 17 18 19 20 21 22 23 24 25 26 27 28 29 30
JAN FEB MAR APR MAY JUN JUL AUG SEP OCT NOV DEC
Sunday Monday Tuesday Wednesday Thursday Friday Saturday

**You can both be right.**

3 4 5 6 7 8 9 10 11 12 13 14 15 16 17 18 19 20 21 22 23 24 25 26 27 28 29 30 31
JAN FEB MAR APR MAY JUN JUL AUG SEP OCT NOV DEC
Sunday Monday Tuesday Wednesday Thursday Friday Saturday

**Focus on commonalities instead of differences.**

1 2 3 4 5 6 7 8 9 10 11 12 13 14 15 16 17 18 19 20 21 22 23 24 25 26 27 28 29 30
JAN FEB MAR APR MAY JUN JUL AUG SEP OCT NOV DEC
Sunday Monday Tuesday Wednesday Thursday Friday Saturday

___

___

___

___

___

___

___

___

___

___

___

___

___

___

___

**Practice being kind to yourself.**

3 4 5 6 7 8 9 10 11 12 13 14 15 16 17 18 19 20 21 22 23 24 25 26 27 28 29 30 31
JAN  FEB  MAR  APR  MAY  JUN  JUL  AUG  SEP  OCT  NOV  DEC
Sunday  Monday  Tuesday  Wednesday  Thursday  Friday  Saturday

**Rehearse how to deal with stressful situations.**

1 2 3 4 5 6 7 8 9 10 11 12 13 14 15 16 17 18 19 20 21 22 23 24 25 26 27 28 29 30
JAN FEB MAR APR MAY JUN JUL AUG SEP OCT NOV DEC
Sunday Monday Tuesday Wednesday Thursday Friday Saturday

**Everything does not deserve a reply.**

3 4 5 6 7 8 9 10 11 12 13 14 15 16 17 18 19 20 21 22 23 24 25 26 27 28 29 30 31
JAN FEB MAR APR MAY JUN JUL AUG SEP OCT NOV DEC
Sunday Monday Tuesday Wednesday Thursday Friday Saturday

**Everyone does not deserve an apology.**

1 2 3 4 5 6 7 8 9 10 11 12 13 14 15 16 17 18 19 20 21 22 23 24 25 26 27 28 29 30
JAN FEB MAR APR MAY JUN JUL AUG SEP OCT NOV DEC
Sunday Monday Tuesday Wednesday Thursday Friday Saturday

**Everything is not an insult.**

3 4 5 6 7 8 9 10 11 12 13 14 15 16 17 18 19 20 21 22 23 24 25 26 27 28 29 30 31
JAN FEB MAR APR MAY JUN JUL AUG SEP OCT NOV DEC
Sunday Monday Tuesday Wednesday Thursday Friday Saturday

**You don't have to forgive everyone.
You can make peace with them instead.**

1 2 3 4 5 6 7 8 9 10 11 12 13 14 15 16 17 18 19 20 21 22 23 24 25 26 27 28 29 30
JAN FEB MAR APR MAY JUN JUL AUG SEP OCT NOV DEC
Sunday Monday Tuesday Wednesday Thursday Friday Saturday

**You don't have to change minds.
Just defend your position.**

3 4 5 6 7 8 9 10 11 12 13 14 15 16 17 18 19 20 21 22 23 24 25 26 27 28 29 30 31
JAN FEB MAR APR MAY JUN JUL AUG SEP OCT NOV DEC
Sunday Monday Tuesday Wednesday Thursday Friday Saturday

**Recognize how different people send and receive information.**

1 2 3 4 5 6 7 8 9 10 11 12 13 14 15 16 17 18 19 20 21 22 23 24 25 26 27 28 29 30
JAN FEB MAR APR MAY JUN JUL AUG SEP OCT NOV DEC
Sunday Monday Tuesday Wednesday Thursday Friday Saturday

___

**Sometimes be unpredictable.**

3 4 5 6 7 8 9 10 11 12 13 14 15 16 17 18 19 20 21 22 23 24 25 26 27 28 29 30 31
JAN FEB MAR APR MAY JUN JUL AUG SEP OCT NOV DEC
Sunday Monday Tuesday Wednesday Thursday Friday Saturday

**Find your "step one".**

1 2 3 4 5 6 7 8 9 10 11 12 13 14 15 16 17 18 19 20 21 22 23 24 25 26 27 28 29 30
JAN  FEB  MAR  APR  MAY  JUN  JUL  AUG  SEP  OCT  NOV  DEC
Sunday  Monday  Tuesday  Wednesday  Thursday  Friday  Saturday

_____

_____

_____

_____

_____

_____

_____

_____

_____

_____

_____

_____

_____

_____

_____

_____

**Recognize the difference between facts and emotions.**

3 4 5 6 7 8 9 10 11 12 13 14 15 16 17 18 19 20 21 22 23 24 25 26 27 28 29 30 31
JAN  FEB  MAR  APR  MAY  JUN  JUL  AUG  SEP  OCT  NOV  DEC
Sunday  Monday  Tuesday  Wednesday  Thursday  Friday  Saturday

**Never give anyone permission to make you feel sad or inferior.**

1 2 3 4 5 6 7 8 9 10 11 12 13 14 15 16 17 18 19 20 21 22 23 24 25 26 27 28 29 30
JAN FEB MAR APR MAY JUN JUL AUG SEP OCT NOV DEC
Sunday Monday Tuesday Wednesday Thursday Friday Saturday

_____

_____

_____

_____

_____

_____

_____

_____

_____

_____

_____

_____

_____

_____

_____

_____

**Take responsibility for your actions.**

3 4 5 6 7 8 9 10 11 12 13 14 15 16 17 18 19 20 21 22 23 24 25 26 27 28 29 30 31
JAN FEB MAR APR MAY JUN JUL AUG SEP OCT NOV DEC
Sunday Monday Tuesday Wednesday Thursday Friday Saturday

**Be a leader when no one else will.**

1 2 3 4 5 6 7 8 9 10 11 12 13 14 15 16 17 18 19 20 21 22 23 24 25 26 27 28 29 30
JAN FEB MAR APR MAY JUN JUL AUG SEP OCT NOV DEC
Sunday Monday Tuesday Wednesday Thursday Friday Saturday

**Be a good follower.**

3 4 5 6 7 8 9 10 11 12 13 14 15 16 17 18 19 20 21 22 23 24 25 26 27 28 29 30 31
JAN FEB MAR APR MAY JUN JUL AUG SEP OCT NOV DEC
Sunday Monday Tuesday Wednesday Thursday Friday Saturday

**Don't repeat the same mistake.**

1 2 3 4 5 6 7 8 9 10 11 12 13 14 15 16 17 18 19 20 21 22 23 24 25 26 27 28 29 30
JAN FEB MAR APR MAY JUN JUL AUG SEP OCT NOV DEC
Sunday Monday Tuesday Wednesday Thursday Friday Saturday

_____

_____

_____

_____

_____

_____

_____

_____

_____

_____

_____

_____

_____

_____

**Be honest with yourself and others.**

3 4 5 6 7 8 9 10 11 12 13 14 15 16 17 18 19 20 21 22 23 24 25 26 27 28 29 30 31
JAN FEB MAR APR MAY JUN JUL AUG SEP OCT NOV DEC
Sunday Monday Tuesday Wednesday Thursday Friday Saturday

**Have integrity.**

1 2 3 4 5 6 7 8 9 10 11 12 13 14 15 16 17 18 19 20 21 22 23 24 25 26 27 28 29 30
JAN FEB MAR APR MAY JUN JUL AUG SEP OCT NOV DEC
Sunday Monday Tuesday Wednesday Thursday Friday Saturday

**Behave in honor even when no one is watching.**

3 4 5 6 7 8 9 10 11 12 13 14 15 16 17 18 19 20 21 22 23 24 25 26 27 28 29 30 31
JAN FEB MAR APR MAY JUN JUL AUG SEP OCT NOV DEC
Sunday Monday Tuesday Wednesday Thursday Friday Saturday

**Live by moral and ethical principles.**

1 2 3 4 5 6 7 8 9 10 11 12 13 14 15 16 17 18 19 20 21 22 23 24 25 26 27 28 29 30
JAN FEB MAR APR MAY JUN JUL AUG SEP OCT NOV DEC
Sunday Monday Tuesday Wednesday Thursday Friday Saturday

**Have personal courage: the ability to face
fear, danger, and adversity.**

3 4 5 6 7 8 9 10 11 12 13 14 15 16 17 18 19 20 21 22 23 24 25 26 27 28 29 30 31
JAN FEB MAR APR MAY JUN JUL AUG SEP OCT NOV DEC
Sunday Monday Tuesday Wednesday Thursday Friday Saturday

**Don't be afraid to be wrong.**

1 2 3 4 5 6 7 8 9 10 11 12 13 14 15 16 17 18 19 20 21 22 23 24 25 26 27 28 29 30
JAN FEB MAR APR MAY JUN JUL AUG SEP OCT NOV DEC
Sunday Monday Tuesday Wednesday Thursday Friday Saturday

**Don't be afraid to agree with an adversary.**

3 4 5 6 7 8 9 10 11 12 13 14 15 16 17 18 19 20 21 22 23 24 25 26 27 28 29 30 31
JAN FEB MAR APR MAY JUN JUL AUG SEP OCT NOV DEC
Sunday Monday Tuesday Wednesday Thursday Friday Saturday

**Lead with a smile.**

1 2 3 4 5 6 7 8 9 10 11 12 13 14 15 16 17 18 19 20 21 22 23 24 25 26 27 28 29 30
JAN  FEB  MAR  APR  MAY  JUN  JUL  AUG  SEP  OCT  NOV  DEC
Sunday  Monday  Tuesday  Wednesday  Thursday  Friday  Saturday

**Never let anyone or anything steal your joy.**

3 4 5 6 7 8 9 10 11 12 13 14 15 16 17 18 19 20 21 22 23 24 25 26 27 28 29 30 31
JAN  FEB  MAR  APR  MAY  JUN  JUL  AUG  SEP  OCT  NOV  DEC
Sunday  Monday  Tuesday  Wednesday  Thursday  Friday  Saturday

**Live well and be your best self.**

1 2 3 4 5 6 7 8 9 10 11 12 13 14 15 16 17 18 19 20 21 22 23 24 25 26 27 28 29 30
JAN FEB MAR APR MAY JUN JUL AUG SEP OCT NOV DEC
Sunday Monday Tuesday Wednesday Thursday Friday Saturday

_____

_____

_____

_____

_____

_____

_____

_____

_____

_____

_____

_____

_____

_____

**Have faith in yourself and your abilities.**

3 4 5 6 7 8 9 10 11 12 13 14 15 16 17 18 19 20 21 22 23 24 25 26 27 28 29 30 31
JAN FEB MAR APR MAY JUN JUL AUG SEP OCT NOV DEC
Sunday Monday Tuesday Wednesday Thursday Friday Saturday

**Smile, even when you don't want to.**

1 2 3 4 5 6 7 8 9 10 11 12 13 14 15 16 17 18 19 20 21 22 23 24 25 26 27 28 29 30
JAN FEB MAR APR MAY JUN JUL AUG SEP OCT NOV DEC
Sunday Monday Tuesday Wednesday Thursday Friday Saturday

**Ask for help and learn to accept help.**

3 4 5 6 7 8 9 10 11 12 13 14 15 16 17 18 19 20 21 22 23 24 25 26 27 28 29 30 31
JAN FEB MAR APR MAY JUN JUL AUG SEP OCT NOV DEC
Sunday Monday Tuesday Wednesday Thursday Friday Saturday

**When you choose your path, you get everything that goes with it.**

1 2 3 4 5 6 7 8 9 10 11 12 13 14 15 16 17 18 19 20 21 22 23 24 25 26 27 28 29 30
JAN FEB MAR APR MAY JUN JUL AUG SEP OCT NOV DEC
Sunday Monday Tuesday Wednesday Thursday Friday Saturday

**Never take ownership of things that don't belong to you.**

3 4 5 6 7 8 9 10 11 12 13 14 15 16 17 18 19 20 21 22 23 24 25 26 27 28 29 30 31
JAN FEB MAR APR MAY JUN JUL AUG SEP OCT NOV DEC
Sunday Monday Tuesday Wednesday Thursday Friday Saturday

**Be patient.**

1 2 3 4 5 6 7 8 9 10 11 12 13 14 15 16 17 18 19 20 21 22 23 24 25 26 27 28 29 30
JAN FEB MAR APR MAY JUN JUL AUG SEP OCT NOV DEC
Sunday Monday Tuesday Wednesday Thursday Friday Saturday

**Learn how to take a joke.**

3 4 5 6 7 8 9 10 11 12 13 14 15 16 17 18 19 20 21 22 23 24 25 26 27 28 29 30 31
JAN FEB MAR APR MAY JUN JUL AUG SEP OCT NOV DEC
Sunday Monday Tuesday Wednesday Thursday Friday Saturday

**Recognize sarcasm.**

1 2 3 4 5 6 7 8 9 10 11 12 13 14 15 16 17 18 19 20 21 22 23 24 25 26 27 28 29 30
JAN FEB MAR APR MAY JUN JUL AUG SEP OCT NOV DEC
Sunday Monday Tuesday Wednesday Thursday Friday Saturday

**The "what" is more important than the "why".**

# About Me

Master Sergeant (MSG) Erinn Watkins is an accomplished Army Veteran with an impressive military resume spanning nearly 30 years. She was one of the first women to become an Army Pathfinder, she helped test and develop important military equipment and programs, and she turned around on the ladder to success to help mentor younger Soldiers on the same path. Now retired, Erinn is proud to be a Pathfinder in a new way – she's reclaimed her power after a turbulent career and leaned into a new mission: showing others how she survived it all.

"Throughout my military career I dealt with a lot of hostility and conflict. I dealt with a lot of toxic people and despite this, I was still very successful. My last few years in the military were … the most mentally challenging thing I had ever experienced. But using my previous experiences, I managed to come out on top. I want to show people how I did this."

Adding "Author" to an already-impressive resume, Erinn's new book *PathfYnder* takes readers on an illuminating and empowering journey to finding their best selves. Leveraging her own experiences – no story is off limits – Erinn lays the path to navigating hostile work environments, toxic leadership, and more.

Erinn has been showing people the best path to success nearly her entire life. Away from the Army, Erinn is a well-known dance instructor (@PetitePrincess on YouTube), teaching styles like Soul Line Dance, Chicago Steppin', and more. Her signature style of instruction helps students to learn quickly while still having a great time.

As a 100% disabled Veteran, Erinn spends her time giving back. She joined the American Legion in 2017, served as the Adjutant of Post 202 in North Carolina, and was on the cover of the Legion Magazine in 2018. Most recently, she's now a Veteran Mentor for the local Veterans Treatment Court.

Erinn has one son, a graduate of Embry Riddle Aeronautical University. She currently resides in Nashville, Tennessee.

info@erinnspeaks.com
www.ErinnSpeaks.com

# Verdelite Publishing, LLC

At Verdelite Publishing, LLC, our goal is to bring your story to life. We are a veteran-friendly publishing house, committed to helping you turn your story into a reality. Whether you're a budding author or a seasoned writer, we are here to help.

We understand the power of storytelling and the impact it has on the reader. Our goal is to bring these stories to life in an honest and meaningful way. Whether you are an aspiring author or a seasoned veteran, Verdelite Publishing, LLC is here to help you share your story. Get in touch with us today to start your journey.

VerdelitePublishing@pm.me

Printed in the USA
CPSIA information can be obtained
at www.ICGtesting.com
JSHW062233041023
49305JS00013B/159